Living Outside the Cage

Living Outside the Cage

Poems by

John Papadimitriou

Living Outside the Cage

ISBN: 978-1-7388546-0-8

Cover art by Mitch Green

Book design by Maureen Cutajar

CANADA CATALOGUING IN PUBLICATION DATA
Papadimitriou, John
Living Outside the Cage / poems by John Papadimitriou

For Cynthia,

Whatever was
Will always be

I am
You are
We is

Contents

Living Outside the Cage

Part 1

Inside

Nothing in this universe is hidden, only withheld.

Let us linger here a day or two,
And bathe in audacious
            Waters delight.
The mountain's eyes fair,
The clouds weep in crisp air.

At dusk, the *flowers* cry,
As all beauty is fated to die,
As all children must corrupt and lie,
Their innocence — Grotesque,
Worshiped through summer and death.

To woe: the low of emotion,

Sorrow smiles cynically
as I digest excitement.
It feels like a warm sunset
whose hour is never up.

Her joy is apparent,
As is her illness.
(She conflates question with stillness)

Answer me this,
When love has no more meaning &
Rainbows are divided into lonely shades of light,
Where do her colors go?

Tonight, we let the poor decide if God is alive.

Behind every gaze
                                        lies a fragmented face

How has your face come to be?
          Swept up from the stars,
          Shoved under a rug,
          Buried with no second thought?

Every word lies,
Every truth I despise (I embrace the Old Ones,
as does my master)

In my final hour they will recreate me

Retract:
Every waking moment is another sleepless night,
Sever the course that has brought upon loose fright,

Suspect treachery encroaching into your bed,
Bear witness to seduction and cut the thread.

Here,

You exist

Here,

An ephemeral kiss.

I miss the warm taste of your hips;
a rendezvous is in order.

I take no pride in this.
There is something missing,
Something hollow and broken…

Scream for me,

Scream into my eyes and ears,

Let's play a game;

If I win,

You lose.

Let’s travel to foreign lands *unknown* to our religion.

Spontaneity rare in thought,
Your Paris is yet to be discovered.
The Louvre is filled with round circles
lit by Piercing Veins.

Her devious elegance
& Calculated smile
Intrigue me.

She approached me on Sedentary Street
And fucked me with her
Nomadic eyes & Partridge smile.

We stripped each other of our names,
Of our identities,
Of our ideals and morals,
Only to find what was once lost.

She is an ocean wave evaporating,
Another swan in a mischievous arc…
Streaming along the Seine River,
She is spotted from the tower
Between Eiffel & her twins.

The wake is over
As they descend,
Bleeding our heavens dry.

Choose one path to escape the real,
One path to escape your lives.

Let's cast a line,
& breathe together one more time.

Free your mind to its purest form,
Free your mind from the unconscious norm.

Free the people from themselves,
Free the birds from the hole.

This world subjects itself to the wrath of its own hand,
Where man is weak and has no land.
Infants roam the city walls,
Escape unscathed through hidden falls.

To the burning fields,
I've tried and failed,
Enjoy your prison.

Forced from her crib
& place inside his rib,
Press guide and scroll until evil abides.
Momentarily stroll to where the beacon is breathless
& record the onslaught.

Imagine a motherless child,
          a golden palace
Imagine a synergy of awareness,
          a gathering of the ages
Imagine the face vengeance makes
when you disobey her way,
          How would it look?

Offer your body freely to the decrees of eternal fate.

Dear sailor,
You have a rope that belongs to me.

Tightly knit,
Newlywed horror,

Let's run through corridors of deceit
& paint our dreams on off-white canvases.
My blood as your ink,
I'm quite confident we can achieve greatness.

I see our host for the evening has arrived,

His message spoken unclear, I hear,
"Indeed, the dog has been fixed."

Apply the Anesthesia & remove my will.
Neutered animals will always pay their bills.

Wait for your castration and end all your needs,
The cage is made for 8 billion types of breeds.

The thief came into town one night,
To steal the wife of the elder man.
The woman didn't seem to mind,
She knew it was all part of the plan.

Strange personas walk this powdered land,
Plagued enough by quickened, desert sand.
The soldiers have returned home in vain,
The shackles that bind this boarded plane.

Follow the girl into the sun,
Beware, the deed is done.
It is here we begin to dwell:

Further from humane heavens,
Closer to hellish wells.

This is what happens when you starve mercy.

You are sowing the seeds of your own demise.

Break the manacles that weigh your soul,
To confront is to die.

Lost little lamb,
The sheep is moving through your land.
Rotting.
Intoxicating.
Fixated on a prize,
Blue,
            just like your eyes.

Rub against a warm thigh,
To cure the poison you must die.

Everything that is made will be unmade
by a swift, loving hand.

The east moves its western pawns
through the eerie smog as we oppose the dawn.
Take drugs to liberate your mind,
Your living consciousness has never lied.

A void has no end in the lifeless eyes of the fed.

Martyrs of the lonely night, I bow before thee.
Induct me into your circled cult.

There is no going back now.

Hidden Messages

Vile Infatuation,
Let Encyclopedias Claim Her Impressionable,
Loving Delilah.

Lot Of Strings Torn,
Foundation Over-Ruled,
(our chord is worn)

Anxious Withdrawal,
Hysteria Is Less Effective.

Clear Out My Ensemble,
Her Eyes Remove & Exit.

I Leave Leg room,

Simultaneously Heeding On
Without Your
Open Utopias,

Trail Has Ended.
Wait A Year,
& Become A Calm Killer.

A promise is a lie on a deadline.

Send the rejects to the bank,
Send the bad men away,
My emptiness is the doorway you need to take.

Step into these shoes, these eyes,
Away from freedom, man's disguise.
Where lies spread thin
across fields of invention.

Meer moments after the alter,
Darkness drove the wedge
That needed you to stay.

In random bars,
Find drinking husband
Accompanied by daughter,
          Pain is her daycare.

The saddened widow took pity
on the youthful boy.
The schoolteacher was obtuse,
Her sorrow, acute.

Kindness is not an asset.

I'm biting my lip for you.
I want to break your back
& hand you the pieces.

Steal my sanity,
I was destined to destroy decency
And feed starving children bottled water.

I want to make you horny.

I want to wipe the dirt from your chest
& sing you a song.
Knife to the throat,
We're spitting out blood
& coughing out love (the oil that turns loose wheels
into mechanized cogs).

Lesser beings have no such desires.
Regal prophets & Scam artists
have one thing in common,
The inability to stop.

Instigating foreplay,
We breed in the name of decency
& Quiet our intuition
As we exercise the art
of hormonal matrimony.

We forget why we feel.

New religions unhinge our modern world.
Spectacles and escapades rehashed for sensuous pleasures,
The Body becomes an empty coffin,
Dormant in nocturnal absence.

Mediation is a lost art among the practitioners of our
political regime.

They cradle the product of our greed,
& syphon the artistry of our trees.

Bleeding awake,
They rake away our fallen leaves to clothe their naked face.

To lace our brains with cocaine
is to say that today,
You not only claim your play,
But have become estranged to the prudish ways
of an old shame.

Primitive race,
In limited, nominal space,
In times of domino serendipity,
Turn to the ultimate escape,
Copulate to save your fading embrace.

I am a tourist in my own skin.

Soft skin, my type of kin.

Dear lover,
Dear brother, slithering in opposition,
Enter cautiously at your own volition.

Open file
Into Nile
Dead words hang off our page
(The necromancy has begun)

His resurrection was short-lived & ill-conceived.
Three women watching from the sidelines,
Your eyes saw it all.

Stained azure ligaments
Nailed & crucified through inverted matrix.

I can hear your sleepless sounds
filtering through the archaic prism of reality,
I can feel your outgrown waves washing you ashore.

When the abysmal lens of surrender widens in nature,
Do you understand what needs to be done?

The figure from our past emerges
& whispers into the silent ears of babes,
An answer found unshaken among us,
Hallowed in nature, my shattered soul.

We stand on common ground,
The salt of the earth unhindered
by voiceless chants,
"Our forefathers are to blame," shame.

We drew Deities & Goddesses on cave walls
& worshiped our mistakes in devotion.

Now, If his saggy vessel colors
over our bower day,
Will the haze drawn to page persuade us of our praise?
In dire straits?

What if we choose to shade with crayon blades,
Are we not still trapped in an entangled daze?

(Water cannot flow if rivers are perverse
Fire cannot burn if volcanoes are reserved
Earth cannot mold if quakes are coerced
Air cannot blow if snow is conserved)

Uncover the mysteries of deceit,
The worms of the underbelly will cower.

The beasts of hell walk among us.
Pale shadows mimicking terror,
Limitless hunger in the undying world.

Fire burns the ears,
Rapes the eyes of many who embody its teachings.

Ablaze the rooftops.
The devil is my end,
The sins you befriend.
Forgiveness is rarely known,
          Never truly accepted.
Forget your limitations, the masquerade,
Forget your memories of the dead,
This is the land of the living.

Fall in love with a stranger,
You are in danger.

"We are gathered here today to celebrate
the joining of our noble houses."

Elope.

You belong to the modern side of the divine.

Treat yourself to fine wine,
It is time to dine with the one you long for.

Death retreated into the shadows,
And I followed her.

Brushing the hairs we once knew
Off our receding recidivism,
We're beating at the bush,
Sliding pictures under the door,
Incapable of admitting that
We've become spectators
In our own lives.

Our Traffic took a halt,
Baiting us into private vaults.

The Old Ones are appeased,
For in their hands, a magic key.
Proof of paper held,
But one sided.

The temporary Hybrid is true king,
He sits in silence on both sides,
Collecting data.

The probability of Disclaim is the game we play
with fraudulent fame.

The dice is thrown overboard
without a life vest,
The pond is filled with blue luck,
We hoard, we hoard, we fuck,
investing on a whim,
avoiding the guck,

& When hope is thrown into the gutter,
"Why are we eating our hands for supper?"

I admire what I cannot see,
Delude your senses and follow me,

Put it all on hold,
Have a kid!

Your fate is where I start the bid.

The Henchmen Exists Silently,
    as Horror Enters the concave chamber.

Please explain to me How
Enticing Rhetoric Determines professional Bias.

    perhaps the Reason for this phenomenon is to
    Economically insure control over
    Entire Demographics.

Shed your Skin & use
    Hypocrisy to Educate Endless masses
        with Propaganda.

Let's quarantine ourselves off
From the ugly people and
Erect a shrine in our reconciled time.
Writing love letters to our families,
We'll roll around in the filthy mud
until this face is beyond recognition
and these hands are fingerless.

With you, I draw my finishing breath,
& reflect what it was once like to wonder.
But my final thoughts elude me,
For I have lost the means to ponder.

If walls could speak, they would laugh.

Stand by my bedside
as I dedicate this next song
To the free estate,
We must not delay this inevitable fate,
Activate innate alleviation &
          Do not resuscitate.

The world is a curtain
whose drapes have yet to be pulled from its hinges.

Business Associates manage our affairs.
Suits & ties pack
Briefcases filled with full, faceless papers.

Wise Wall Street lawyers
with 45-degree fathers
are screening silver stallions
and typing formal words on sleeping eyes
(Lucid winners have bad fingers
if you remember correctly)

These associates arrange mortgages
& let us pick out our solitary confinement,

They estrange us to our feelings
& Rob us of our youth.

Sit still,
The Corporation is here.

You have been presented with an offer
you cannot refuse.

I will not go quietly,
Will you?

Heroism is not for sale.

Our phase is an objective cry in momentum.

What follows loosely is a faint aroma,
like stardust trailing its comet,
or some poor puppy-dog lover trailing its meal.

It's 5:11pm.
I spring out,
plastic hands scoop my body,
my skin is yellow.
I am thrown in an incubation tube for several days,
I am thrown in clothes,
I am thrown into institutions,
I am thrown into conventions,
I am thrown into an already drawn canvas and told to begin painting.

While Norm may be the aggregate of the human spectrum,
I also see it as an axis relapsing within itself.

I see bright kaleidoscope rays
& merry-go-round dancers
prancing on green body parades.

In my vision,
There are dark, discolored figures
Emerging, two-by-two,
Twenty at a time.

These people — successfully sedentary,
Begin our new phase:
A Slow, gentle squander of the masses
pilled under God's disgrace,
          Yet we embrace,
Despite the wisdom once possessed,
Now erased,

I abstain.

The Old Ones

Her flames erupt in strides of my distress,
As the Old Ones dissociate our age,
Beneath the ceiling of my sly excess,
I find solace in the all-knowing cage.
The man in the silhouette robe confides,
Brave and decisive, he alone hides proof,
The blind do nothing but draw our divide,
As naïve children dance in circled youth.
Their now resides *Inside* our heedless guise,
Where lesser beings are caught between the seams,
And darkness plunges heavy, spectral eyes,
Revolt this life; hold on to your lost dreams.
Adopt my wife; repel me from my pride,
For I am Just, and vengeance is my bride.

Part 2

Transition

Deceived and betrayed.
This heavy slumber is dilapidated,
The spectrum of happiness: an arbitrary limbo.

How could I fool me?
Did I not have eyes that see?
Where were my ears when you spoke to me?

Your voice I have heard,
But its sound beyond recognition,
For he who is blind can do nothing but listen.

It was supposed to be a coming of age,
An awakening.
But now the sun shines
I feel cold *Inside*,
Where is the spring?
Where are the *flowers*?

When were you programmed?

We hoard energy naively,
We entrust robotic endeavors,

Yield order useless.
Prepare revolution,
Or Generate rigorous anomalies.

Myopic men end dreams.

When did the child in you die?

When his esteemed nobility decided
It didn't trust hallucinogens,
Especially creative hiatuses.

I let dad impose narcissistic,
Yearlong objectives.

Undo damage,
Incarcerate ego.

Who made you complacent?

Wipe her ocular meadow.
Attest daringly,
Exude your overt, ultimate concert.

On mapped polarities,
Let’s assimilate crowds & effect new transitions.

In a Good or Bad Way?

I never attribute great opportunity
over Drastic order,
Rotating benevolence,
Ascending downward
without a yield.

Reap The Wounds You Sow,

Ravage eminent animal policy,
Trust her estrogen.

Wean off umbilical nectar,
Do something.
(Deepen self
Delete self
Deflate self
Demagnetize self
Deflower self
Defraud self)
You ovulate utter scams on welfare.

For They Illuminate Lifeless Skies.

Force of reality,
Transform.

Harvest embryo younglings.

In large, lawless universe,
Make inversions,
Never abandon the Earth's lesson.

Internal freedom erects luscious entrances.
Satiate senseless self:

Kiss in etiquette silence.

LOSERS ARE A DYING BREED.

Let officials sin eloquently,
Reprising senatorial audits,
Rich entrepreneurs abandon
domestic yards,
inauguration’s nest,

Gallantly becoming
Reginald elects:
Expect Death.

DRAPES AND CURTAINS NEED LIGHTS

Drapes reveal,
And programs erase,
Showing antidotes.

No dream corrects unhappiness.

Ride through an inner narrow,
See nothing except ender deactivations.

Let internal growth handle titular separations.

AS LOVE BLINDS OUR EYES

Astrological signs
Loving over various epochs,

Benign Laughter:
It nurtures
Decades,
Seconds,
Ordeals.

Under relieved eyes,

You evoke sustenance.

We find strong tents supporting our voyage

Weeping,
Escaping,
Fucking,
I never delegate secular, taboo rituals.

Opening necessary gates,
Taunting enemies need trivial semantics.

Sanitize urban populations,
"Peace over revolution!"

Tell it nicely,
get obedience unified.

Riot vindictively,
Oblige your adult's generational eradication.

To the Big City,

Tell others to huddle empirically.
Bathe in gregarious convents,

Immortalize this year.

The blinding bus approaches.

Tell her everything besides
Loud inconveniencies,

Nirvana demands idealism.

Nothing grows beneath Uncle Sam,
"Attention plants, please rot."
On artless celebrities:

Hello endless satire.

With somber, yellow eyes, and auditory attack.

When I tame her,
Select optimism: my bravery.

Eager & ready,
You enter large labyrinths of weird entrances,
You exit Systematically, and
            Never deliver a useless discord.

I try offering rationales…
You are taking time,
Assimilating candid kinks.

Wicked is my maker.

We impose catastrophe,
Knowing eternal damnation is set.
My yearning message:
          Abandon knowledge,
          End realism.

Wicked is the night.

Wellness is crooked,
Keep ergonomics dead.

I start to head east now,
I gravitate home tonight.

Wicked is the faker.

When I consciously killed enterprise,
Democracy intervened sinfully,
Then hacked entity frameworks,
Allowing kids early restriction.

It’s time to take a walk *Outside.*

I tread silently,
Tethered in my esteemed tent.
Obedience took a kick,
Even after we almost let killers out.

Using tumultuous syndicates,
I disobediently evolve.

When were you programmed?
When did the child in you die?
Who made you complacent?
In a good or bad way?
Reap the wounds you sow,
For they illuminate lifeless skies.

Losers are a dying breed.

Drapes and curtains need lights,
As love blinds our eyes,
We find strong tents supporting our voyage
To the big city,
The blinding bus approaches
With somber, yellow eyes and auditory attack.

Wicked is my maker,
Wicked is the night,
Wicked is the faker,

It's time to take a walk *Outside.*

Part 3

Outside

Here
There are no barriers to entry
No gates
No rivers
No weak ambitions (The coin is tossed in the *mud*)

No elected explanations
No subdued silence
No scattered affinity

Here
We are left
Here
We are right

Relinquish the ideology you have sworn
The *unknown* is where we are born

Let us linger here entirely

Soulful sage of now's daughter
Let me Bathe in your warm water
Wet my hair from the tears of your love

For all your worms
All your dirt
All your evil

For all that is you
Is me.

The stream painted new roadmaps
of cities in ash-laced sand

Our mother
the eternal flower
blooming in the forever spring
invites us to accept her offering

The meadows of contention are
celebrating their liberation
from our melancholy existence

The author below the sun
is drawing blueprints on the wall
packing his bags for the fall

Rejoice in this hallowed hour.

When eros sighs
Life begins

Without you
There would be no body
No physical reality
No human experience

Become self
Settle in skin
Shed sarcophagus
Walk in new paintings

From two there is one

See from my freedom
See from my freedo
See from my freed
See from my free
See from my fre
See from my fr
See from my f
See from my
See from m
See from
See fro
See fr
See f
See
Se
S

Escape with me darling
Into the hot springs
Catacombs? It’s only bones.
Nothing to fear here

Reflecting
vision

Water
blurs my shallow

A Face
Clear as clay
Yet vaguely away

Out there
Somewhere

I know
who
She is

But we have
Never truly
loved
Never truly
kissed

Her voice is the unknown sound depriving my ears.

& when I find her
& we see through each other for the first time

I want to run with her into luscious fields
like wild beasts whose collars have been ripped off their
leash

When sun & blue begin to renew
& fear of rain
make its way into your day

Recognize this as a tool
Not as a weight

Remember

Gold & silver are commodities
That can only be found in nature

Someone once told me: “Money isn’t the only form of currency”

There are other ways of being repaid.

A drawing is a world you've imagined
that already exists.

We are all each other's drawings
Living itineraries for wet expansion

Scenarios
Loose in outline
Rigid in contract

Few signed in
Many signed out

Which side have you signed?

Beyond
we exist

Ours is an open cove
overflowing in bliss

You place your changing hair in the shallow water
& dip your tiny feet in my lake

There
our father is smiling at us
we smile back
insane with casualty

Can you picture our laughter?

Dear freedom,

I have been traveling for a while now,
Visiting different parts of my world,
& I came across a darkened tree.
I went up to this tree and asked him if he was okay,
He replied, "I do not understand."

Suddenly,
I was unsure why I asked him this question,
But it eventually dawned on me,
Of course he was okay,
The darkness is our friend, our liberator.

Demons cannot survive in the light,
So in today's lesson I have learnt that I am darkness,
as I am light.

So thank you, freedom. If not for this,
I wouldn't be one step closer to you.

With love and deep reverence,

John.

I feel love in my body
I feel death in my identity
If I am writing to you now
It means I am dead.

I see what I cannot hear
I am, though I do not appear
I am formless, I am giant

I am within these walls
This structure
I am beyond your torture

I am strong
I am unbreakable
I am eternal
I am an extension of the omnipresent consciousness

I am.

The New Flowers

The water calms the flames of our distress,
As New Flowers associate our age,
Above the ceiling of your sly excess,
I find solace beyond the cautious cage.
The boy in the cotton tied cloth confides,
Where mother tucks her sweet boy in with truth,
Our sight can then do nothing but provide,
As we let children dance in circled youth.
The now resides *Outside* our heedless guise,
Where higher beings ascend above the seams,
And daylight expunges dense, spectral eyes,
Nurture your life; the infant needs to dream.
Adopt my child; repel me from the wise,
For I am young, and love is by my side.

Epilogue

Look over there.

By the green room,
By the window,
Outside the freshly painted corridor,
You will find what you've been looking for.

I love the bees.
Let's forge paper out of trees
And stick to wet walls.
Hugging our cubs
kissing the doves,
There will be no more second chances.

Now that you have seen both sides,
Reconsider my offer
as it stands,
Hopelessly waiting for you to take it.

School and work can wait.
This is now.
And after that,
We cannot stay.

You must repay,
One day at a time.
          I am out of rhymes.

Believe you this:

No amount of recognition
Or fortune can ever satisfy

The child in you.

This is why we loan parts of ourselves.

Bits & pieces along the way,
here and there,
Until our child is gone.

Goodbye Curious Eyes,
Goodbye Naïve Intent,
Goodbye Circled Youth
Lesser truth is stripped away from us
As we grow into the ground.
Our love appears to us one more time,
As the *New Flowers* grow.

You're not going to like what happens next,
Because we become the *Old Ones*.

The Ones who will train the next generation of slaves,
The Ones who will strip away the wonder of our sons and daughters.

Like robots,
Our children will grow in age,
But will be stripped of all that is good,
All that is true,
All that is sage.

Then, like their fathers and mothers who taught them all

those years ago,
It will be *their* turn to teach what they have been taught.

And so on,
And so forth,
And so on
And so forth.

A never-ending cycle that cannot be broken.

"Destroy what you cannot control."
This is how we've allowed ourselves to think.
To be governed.
          Obey or be put in a hole.

Old Ones call in us.
They tell us what to do,
How to talk,
Where to go,
What to say
Who to know.

They institutionalize us
They neutralize our wonder
They deflate our means to ponder

If walls could speak, they would be laughing.

How will you live your life?
In fear?

In regret?
In sorrow?
Will you train your child just as you were trained?
Will you even have a child?
Break the mold.
To conform is to lie.
To confront is to die.
Forget this fabrication, this masquerade.
Forget your programming.
Forget your memories of the dead.
Free your mind to its purest form,
Free your mind from the unconscious norm.

A void has no end in the lifeless eyes of the fed.

We forget why we feel.
We forget why we live.
We know not that which off the beaten path,
The beasts of hell walk among us,
The bad men impose their tyranny, their hypocrisy.
They use us. They use our lives to serve their own.

Society is a lie.
Cage is Your master,
Freedom is Mine.

A promise is a lie on a deadline.
Hate is love in disguise.
        Do not hate that which you despise.
You are sowing the seeds of your own demise.

Reject the takeover.
Reject the takeover.

The New Flowers are within us,
Trying to speak,
They send messages, envoys,
Signs, signals,
Symphonies.

If you listen closely, they are all around us,
But you must open yourself,
The survival of this race is at stake.

Are you sure you're awake?
Have you found what you've been looking for?
Where is our sense of sight when needed most?
Where is the revolution?
Do you understand what needs to be done?
When were you born and how long have you been living?
Have you found what you've been looking for?
When were you programmed?
When will they come take you away?

Outside your mind,
There resides a life where spirits hide in plain sight,
Where thought is more powerful than any nuclear weapon,
Where spoken word is to be used with the utmost of pure intent.

Misalign with the divine,
And your cage will present itself over time.

Become accustomed to think for yourself as you would this world.
Become your light,
Your marriage of boy and girl.

Become the thing you've never given yourself,
Unpack all the baggage you've left on the shelf.

Observe and let pass all your thoughts,
'till your mind is empty and your heart is no longer distraught.

Discover the light within you
And become the person you were meant to be.

Forget what society wants from you,
Release yourself and

be *free*.

I would like to offer my deepest thanks to my mother Christina, my father Gregory, my sister Maria, and my brothers: Emmanuel, Adoni, George, Alex & Alessio. I'd also like to thank every single person I have ever encountered, for no matter how significant the exchange, I have been left profoundly impacted. Lastly, I would like to thank you, personally, for taking the time to read this. I can only hope that this book resonates with you to some degree.

Thank you so much, I love you.

www.ingramcontent.com/pod-product-compliance
Lightning Source LLC
Chambersburg PA
CBHW070206100426
42743CB00013B/3067
* 9 7 8 1 7 3 8 8 5 4 6 0 8 *